Pink Floyd

Captured Through Time

Pink Floyd
Captured Through Time

WYMER
PUBLISHING
Bedford, England

First published in Great Britain in 2019
by Wymer Publishing
www.wymerpublishing.co.uk
Tel: 01234 326691
Wymer Publishing is a trading name of Wymer (UK) Ltd

Copyright © 2019 Wymer Publishing.
This edition published 2021.

ISBN: 978-1-912782-75-8

The Author hereby asserts his rights to be identified
as the author of this work in accordance with sections
77 to 78 of the Copyright, Designs & Patents Act 1988.

All rights reserved. No part of this publication may be
reproduced or transmitted in any form or by any means,
electronic or mechanical, including photocopying, or any
information storage and retrieval system, without written
permission from the publisher.

This publication is sold subject to the condition that it shall not,
by way of trade or otherwise, be lent, re-sold, hired out or
otherwise circulated without the publishers prior consent in any
form of binding or cover other than that in which it is published
and without a similar condition including this condition
being imposed on the subsequent purchaser.

Every effort has been made to trace the copyright holders of the
photographs in this book but some were unreachable. We would
be grateful if the photographers concerned would contact us.

Design by Andy Bishop / 1016 Sarpsborg
Printed and bound in England by Halstan Ltd.

A catalogue record for this book is available from the British Library.

Cover design by 1016 Sarpsborg
Front cover photo © Roger Tillberg / Alamy Stock Photo
Back cover photo © Lee Millward

"One of the great things about the Floyd is the dynamics of the music. You rarely hear those kind of dynamics in a live concert, from quite quiet to a lot of noise; but it's been the Floyd's thing, ever since we started, to have a more subtle balance between quiet and loud. For me, that might possibly have come from being brought up on classical music, in which the symphonies have huge dynamics."
Rick Wright

"My technique is laughable at times. I have developed a style of my own, I suppose, which creeps around… I don't have to have too much technique for it. I've developed the parts of my technique that are useful to me. I'll never be a very fast guitar player. I don't really know what to say about my style. There's always a melodic intent in there."
David Gilmour

"There is no purpose. We do whatever we do. You either blow your brains out or get on with something."
Roger Waters

"What was blindingly obvious pretty early on was that if you were successful you could have more studio time, bigger shows, better equipment and better sound."
Nick Mason

"That's all I wanted to do as a kid. Play a guitar properly and jump around. But too many people got in the way."
Syd Barrett

All Saints Church Hall at Powis Gardens, Notting Hill, London, October 1966.

"It was great when Syd joined. Before him, we'd play the R&B classics, because that's what all groups were supposed to be doing then. With Syd, the direction changed; it became more improvised around the guitar and keyboards. Roger started to play the bass as a lead instrument, and I started to introduce more of my classical feel."
Rick Wright

Graham Keen (Pictorial Press Ltd / Alamy Stock Photo)

At the UFO Club, Tottenham Court Road, London.

The club opened in December 1966 but only ran for a few months until the summer of '67. Floyd played there on a monthly basis with their last performance being on 28th July.

Floyd was part of a benefit carnival for Oxfam at the Royal Albert Hall on 12th December 1966. Earlier in the day they gathered at the Albert Memorial opposite the venue for a bread and water lunch to draw attention to Oxfam's Christmas appeal. Elaine Osborn is serving the bread and water. The full line-up in this shot is (back row, left to right): Syd Barrett, Barry Fantoni, Gordon Waller, Roger Waters, (front row, left to right): Nick Mason, Rick Wright, Paul Jones, Peter Asher and Cat Stevens.

"I first saw Syd playing with Pink Floyd at All Saints Hall, Notting Hill, 1966. The Floyd were on their way to becoming the premier underground group, soon to headline at UFO and the Roundhouse. With our perception of time changed by mind-altering substances, we didn't want two-minute pop songs. Dressed in their Thea Porter silks and lit up like wondrous gargoyles by coloured blobs of oil and water, the Floyd brought us the musical free-fall that we craved. The dark rumble of 'Interstellar Overdrive' would curdle in our blood and lift us into infinite space, and instrumental improvisations could last forty minutes in real time. In between these cosmic journeys there were Syd's exotic ditties about gnomes, mice and the I Ching."
Jenny Fabian, The Guardian, 13 November 2001

Photo credit: Trinity Mirror / Mirrorpix / Alamy Stock photo

March 1967. Not just another run of the mill pop group from EMI's stable.

"For us the most important thing is to be visual, and for the cats watching us to have fun. This is all we want. We get very upset if people get bored when we're only half way through smashing the second set. Then all of a sudden they hear 'Arnold Layne' and they flip all over again."
Roger Waters, Rave, June 1967

"We feel that in the future, groups are going to have to offer much more than just a pop show. They'll have to offer a well-presented theatre show."
Syd Barrett, Melody Maker, September 1967

"On the club scene we rate about two out of ten and 'must try harder.' "We've had problems with our equipment and we can't get the P.A. to work because we play extremely loudly. It's a pity because Syd writes great lyrics and nobody ever hears them."
Roger Waters, Melody Maker, August, 1967

Backstage at London's Saville Theatre, 1st October 1967.

The expressions on the band's faces were often matched by some of the audiences at that time. Particularly at Cesar's Club in Bedford later the same month.

Despite having already played Bedford the previous year, this concert was advertised in the Bedford Record as Pink Lloyd! Having already secured a top twenty hit with 'Arnold Layne', the follow up 'See Emily Play' was an even bigger hit, which made number six and saw the band performing on Top Of The Pops a couple of months before this show. Both singles were relatively commercial and would undoubtedly have been instrumental in drawing the Bedford fans to this concert.

Debut album *The Piper At The Gates Of Dawn* had also been released in August, and the group was generally well received but much of their live set wasn't particularly reflective of the studio recordings. Whilst some critics raved about them, it wasn't quite the same with Bedford's music goers.

Local journalist Steve Peacock recalled this gig in the seventies for *Sounds* and commented: "I remember seeing them play an aggressive set to a cowed audience. They seemed to take a gloomy kind of pleasure in it. In the dressing-cupboard afterwards, Roger Waters made the grim comment, 'at least we frightened a few people tonight'."

Syd Barrett was already becoming more erratic with each day as a result of excessive LSD use. His mental health was suffering and it is widely reported that at several gigs he struggled with the concept of playing guitar and singing at the same time. Was the Bedford gig one of those nights where Barrett's performance significantly affected the band?

One thing we do know is that Dennis Chamberlain, lead guitarist with Bedford's own Little Women who supported Floyd on this evening remembers Barrett leaving his guitar behind. Dennis was seriously considering whether or not to take it home with him when suddenly Barrett returned at the last minute to reclaim his instrument!

SIX GREAT GROUPS IN JUNE AT CESAR'S, BEDFORD
(ADJOINING LEE WEST BOWLING CENTRE LONDON ROAD)
JUNE 9—FREDDIE MAC AND THE MAC SOUND (16-piece Big Band Continuous show)
JUNE 10—THE MERSEYS features TWO LEAD SINGERS
JUNE 16—The Controversial MARMALADE
JUNE 17—THE FAMILY—BIG BRASS SOUND
JUNE 23—BILLY J. KRAMER AND THE DAKOTAS
JUNE 24—PINK FLOYD (THE GREATEST)
FRIDAY NITE 5/- :: SATURDAY NITE 7/6
TOP D.J.'s FROM BRITAIN and U.S.A.

READERS' LETTERS

The Pink Floyd

Sir,—In reply to John Gillett's letter, which you published on November 7, I would like to say that he was not speaking for me when he said that Bedfordshire youth have more intelligence than to watch and to listen to "such trash" as the Pink Floyd. I agree with Discspinner that his group were brilliant. I am also in favour of the light shows the Pink Floyd have in their act—they blend with the so-called psychadelic music.

Some people do like to watch the groups perform, and not just dance all night. If that is all people want to do they may as well play records. I would like to see the Pink Floyd come back to Bedford but they are not likely to after the way in which they were treated. It is no wonder we do not get many top groups in Bedford—half the people do not know what it is all about.

TERRY O'BRIEN.
104 Mile Road,
Bedford.

The 'scene'

Sir,—In reply to letters about Bedford's "dead scene", we would like to say that the West End Club, Bedford, possess the finest dance hall in Bedford and Bedfordshire—and we can assure the writers of the letters that there is no "dead scene" here. If those who travel to Northampton, Luton, or Stevenage care to come and see they will find between 300 and 400 happy dancers, of all ages, every weekend.

L. J. HENWOOD.
(President)
D. M. PURDY
(Secretary)
West End Club,
Bedford.

Why did they go?

Why, oh why, did half the people at Cesar's Club, Bedford, melt away, I know not where, while the Pink Floyd, that brilliant band of experimental electronic musicians, were only part-way through their act last week?

It wasn't because the act was badly presented, so perhaps it was because the musical tastes of Bedfordians are very different from those of the rest of the country. Or maybe they were all called Cinderella and had to be home by midnight.

If Cesar's are going to maintain this high standard of performers, complaints about the "Dead Bedford scene" may fade a bit.

LETTERS

Mistaken

Sir,—Discspinner asked on October 24 why half the people walked out of Cesar's Club, Bedford, during the performance of the Pink Floyd two weeks ago. It was not, as he suggested, because they were a load of Cinderellas who had to be home by midnight, on the contrary, they would probably have stayed all night but they were disgusted at having paid good money to listen to such trash.

If the promoters (and the group) think that the youth of Bedfordshire haven't the intelligence to appreciate better pop music than that they are very mistaken.

Discspinner might also like to know that we go to dances to dance, not to stand around all night drinking "Cokes" and watching someone at the back of the hall trying to be artistic with the lighting.

JOHN GILLETT,
16 Lea Road,
Ampthill.

"The first time I saw Syd was when Pink Floyd played the All Saints Hall, Notting Hill in 1966. I was blown away. They were a great band, and the slide-show was something one had never seen before. They were the soundtrack to the underground, emblematic of its spirit and mood. And by May '67, they'd put the underground onto their shoulders, and taken it into the mainstream. Syd's contribution to that was that he wrote the songs, he sang lead, he played lead guitar. In any other band, he would have been the absolute focus. But because the Floyd's style of presentation was so anonymous, with everybody merging into this red and pink flashing light, he never really took the role of leader."
Joe Boyd

"It all went off the rails in the autumn '67 on their first US tour. I flew out ahead of the band and went to see our agent in New York, a guy called Gimpy. He gave me all the contacts for the shows – two in San Francisco with Bill Graham, one at the Cheetah Club in Santa Monica, one more somewhere and TV slots on the Perry Como and Pat Boone shows and on American Bandstand. Then he opened a drawer and offered me a gun, which he said I'd need on tour. I politely declined and flew to 'Frisco unarmed to meet Bill Graham. We missed the first Fillmore West gig, as they had no visas. Bill rang the US ambassador in London at about 4am, got him out of bed and screamed at him to get the visas sorted. They came through and the band arrived. But they were totally dysfunctional from the start. Basically, Syd wasn't playing anything. He had a whistle, which he'd blow from time to time. The tour should have been fantastic. There I was sharing a bottle of Southern Comfort with Janis Joplin. But it was miserable. Nobody was talking to Syd. I had to chaperone him everywhere to prevent anything too dreadful happening to him."
Andrew King

"In America it was a lot grittier because they were fighting a war. I think it was very short lived, the whole Summer of Love because it became commercial almost instantly. The period of free concerts and all the rest of it was very brief before it became, "hang on, this band could sell a million albums.""
Nick Mason, The Drummer's Journal, Issue Six, Spring 2014

"You're trying to be in this band… and things aren't really working out and you don't really understand why. You can't believe that someone's deliberately trying to screw it up and yet the other half of you is saying, This man's crazy – he's trying to destroy me!' "
Nick Mason

"Syd was so beautiful with his violet eyes. I only sort of laid beside him, nothing more could be accomplished. Then he had a breakdown and was gone. He hardly spoke. He would just tolerate me because I was so overpowered, so in awe that I didn't really speak either. I only hung around him for two or three weeks just before he flipped and was virtually removed from the group. I knew Syd was wonderful because he wrote such wonderful songs. He didn't have to speak because the fact that he couldn't speak made him who he was: this person who wrote these mysterious songs. I just liked looking at him: he was very pretty. A lot of the time with pop stars, when they open their mouths, it was all completely ruined anyway. So it was perfect that he was like that. My first pop star and it was just wonderful that he didn't speak."

Jenny Fabian, Groupie, 1969

"Factually, we started during the late '60s with the psychedelic music, a period that was known as experimental as far as drugs were concerned. The Pink Floyd were in the middle of that culture, so everyone naturally assumed that we were also doing drugs. But that wasn't the case. In Syd Barrett's case it was, but not in our case. I think that music was our drug. Of course, we all did drugs here and there in social events, but I've tried only once in my life before a show, and it was marijuana. We went onstage, I think it was in Paris in '68, and I couldn't play a single note. Actually, I did manage to play one note. It's a mistake thinking that drugs supplied Pink Floyd with the inspiration. The ones who took drugs were the ones who came to see the shows."

Rick Wright, 8 November 1996

On 30th April 1968 Floyd performed for Dutch TV prior to a planned opening night of a Dutch tour at the Paradiso in Amsterdam, however the gig was postponed and rescheduled. Throughout May and June they played several shows in the Netherlands interspersed with gigs and recording sessions in England.

Photos: Laurens van Houten (Frank White Photo Agency)

The last four photos from the Netherlands come from the last date of the tour at the Houtrusthallen in The Hague, on the first of a two day festival with other bands including The Small Faces and The Pretty Things. The festival was given the grandiose name of The 1st Holiness Kitschgarten For The Liberation of Love & Peace in Colours.

Even though it was billed as the 21st June, Floyd didn't take the stage until 4:00 in the morning of the 22nd for a short set before heading back to England and a show that evening at the University of East Anglia in Norwich with Fairport Convention.

Photos: Laurens van Houten (Frank White Photo Agency)

At Steve Paul's The Scene New York, July 1968 during the band's second US tour and the first with Dave Gilmour. The band played three nights at the Manhattan Club and were supported by Fleetwood Mac for the first of these and by the John Hammond Trio for the other two.

Pictorial Press Ltd / Alamy Stock Photos

Victoria Rooms, Bristol University, 3rd March 1969.

Like many shows of the time this was billed as a dance gig but Floyd's audience was happy to just sit and absorb the music.

Photos: Tony Byers (Alamy Stock Photo)

A highly animated Roger Waters and a chilled Nick Mason at the Theatre des Champs-Elysées, Elysée, Paris, January 1970

"We were never that mad about being called psychedelic, that was a very brief period. Saying that, music is whatever you believe it to be and if people wanted to take LSD and trip to our music so be it, but it wasn't written in that way."
Nick Mason, The Drummer's Journal, Issue Six, Spring 2014

Roger Tillberg (Alamy Stock Photo)

Sweden, March 1970

Holland Pop Festival, Kralingse Bos, Rotterdam on 28th June 1970.

This concert was billed as the Dutch Woodstock and a film called Stamping Ground was released.

Photos: Laurens van Houten (Frank White Photo Agency)

Concertgebouw, Amsterdam, 6th November 1970.

Photos: Laurens van Houten (Frank White Photo Agency)

"I could have been an architect, but I don't think I'd have been very happy, I hated being under the boot."
Roger Waters, 1970

The following night November 7th at the Grote Zaal, De Doelen, Rotterdam,

Laurens van Houten (Frank White Photo Agency)

Photo: Laurens van Houten (Frank White Photo Agency)

Photos: Laurens van Houten (Frank White Photo Agency)

Photo: Laurens van Houten (Frank White Photo Agency)

Photos: Laurens van Houten (Frank White Photo Agency)

Photos: Laurens van Houten (Frank White Photo Agency)

"I don't think I'm easy to talk about. I've got a very irregular head. And I'm not anything that you think I am anyway."
Sid Barrett,
Rolling Stone, December 1971

Photos: Laurens van Houten (Frank White Photo Agency)

Photo: Laurens van Houten (Frank White Photo Agency)

Photo: Laurens van Houten (Frank White Photo Agency)

Roger at the Garden Party concert at Crystal Palace Bowl, 15th May 1971.

The bill was completed with Quiver, Mountain and The Faces. This concert saw the debut of a new piece called 'The Return Of The Son Of Nothing' which soon became known as 'Echoes'.

The finale of the concert featured orange smoke bombs, fireworks and a giant rubber octopus which was in the pool in front of the stage. According to photographer Robert Ellis the fish in the pond were killed by smoke flares set off underwater. "They were trying to inflate the octopus which had been damaged from the many people who splashed around in it earlier. Stirring up the bottom of the pond also killed off the water lilies!"

Rick Wright at the Music Hall, Boston, Massachusetts, 4th May 1972.

The gig was originally to be at the Orpheum Theatre but was switched to the bigger hall due to ticket demand. The concerts at this time included *Dark Side Of The Moon* even though it was still nearly a year before it was released.

Jim Kozlowski (Frank White Photo Agency)

David Gilmour at the Amsterdam Rock Circus, Olympisch Stadium, Amsterdam, The Netherlands, 22 May 1972.

Some film footage of this show emerged in recent years. The performance started with an orchestra-less 'Atom Heart Mother' which was to be the last time it was performed.

EEN VERBIJSTERENDE SHOW, MET UITSTEKENDE POPGROEPEN, CIRCUS ACTS, CAN-CAN-DANSERESSEN EN TAL VAN ONVERWACHTE GEBEURTENISSEN

Tweede pinksterdag, 22 mei a.s. in het Olympisch Stadion te Amsterdam, van 12 uur 's middags tot 12 uur 's nachts

PINK FLOYD – DONOVAN – GENE CLARK – SPENCER DAVIS & SNEAKY PETE – DR. JOHN THE NIGHTTRIPPER
TOM PAXTON – BUDDY MILES – MEMPHIS SLIM – NEW RIDERS OF THE PURPLE SAGE – PACIFIC GAS AND ELECTRIC
SGT. PEPPERS BAND – HET GEWESTELIJK ORKEST – JOE LIGHT' LICHTSHOW EN VELE GROTE VERRASSINGEN

Toegangsprijs: in de voorverkoop f 15,50 (tijdens het festival aan de kassa f 17,—

LET OP: tijdens de show kun je rustig rondwandelen als je dat wilt.
Ook op de grasmat en op het terrein binnen de hekken van het Stadion.
De show zal ook zichtbaar zijn middels 2 video-schermen van 9 × 12 meter

KAARTVERKOOP AAN ONDERSTAANDE VERKOOPADRESSEN:

Alkmaar	Arnhem	Delft	Groningen	Hilversum	Nijmegen	Utrecht
ma, Langestr. 73,	Popshop,	Hees n.v. Popcorner,	Fa. Hemmes,	Wessels,	Nijm. Muziekhandel,	NOZ,
200 - 1 73 43	Varkensstr. 40,	Choorstr.,	Steentilstr. 28,	Langestr. 59 g,	Grote Markt 35,	Amsterdamsestraatwe
Amersfoort	085 - 43 36 41	015 - 2 48 83	050 - 12 85 03	02150 - 4 24 35	08800 - 2 18 38	030 - 44 08 80
Muziekhandel Veerman,	**Assen**	**Dordrecht**	**Den Haag**	**Leeuwarden**	**Rotterdam**	**Venlo**
Arnhemseweg 32,	Andre's Platenbar,	Spiering,	Caminada,	v. d. Akker,	Dankers,	Dom v. d. Berg,
3490 - 1 30 27	Brink 20,	Voorstr. 382,	Plaats 17,	Nieuwestad 39,	Coolsingel 47,	Vleesstr. 43,
Amsterdam	05920 - 1 51 56	01850 - 3 34 31	070 - 60 99 00	05100 - 2 63 37	010 - 13 50 95	04700 - 1 48 18
Nieuwe Muziekhandel,	**Den Bosch**	**Eindhoven**	**Haarlem**	**Leiden**	**DISK**	**Vlissingen**
Leidsestraat 52,	Frans de Kok,	Fa. v. Leest,	MIC,	MIC,	v. Oldenbarneveldpl.	Meul Meester,
020 - 23 73 21	Pensmarkt 15,	Herman Boexstr. 12,	Gr. Houtstr. 62,	Haarlemmerstr. 139 a,	010 - 14 78 42	St. Jacobstr. 13,
Apeldoorn	04100 - 3 96 51	040 - 6 58 59	023 - 32 75 59	01710 - 4 96 97		01184 - 26 36
Radiohuis Jeths	**Breda**	**Enschede**	**Den Helder**	**Maastricht**	**Tilburg**	**Zwolle**
Hoofdstr./Hofstr.	Muziekhandel Spronk,	Demoed's Muziekhandel,	Blok's Grammofoonpl.	De Harp,	Frans de Kok,	De Artiest,
5760 - 1 42 50	Torenstr. 21,	Haaksbergerstr. 20,	Keizerstr. 55,	Spilstr. 13,	Heuvelstr. 104,	Luttekestr. 5,
	01600 - 3 87 09	05420 - 2 46 83	02230 - 1 38 08	043 - 1 84 88	04250 - 3 34 70	05200 - 1 17 77

Merriweather Post Pavilion, Columbia, Maryland in June 1973.

Images / Alamy Stock Photo (courtesy US National Archives)

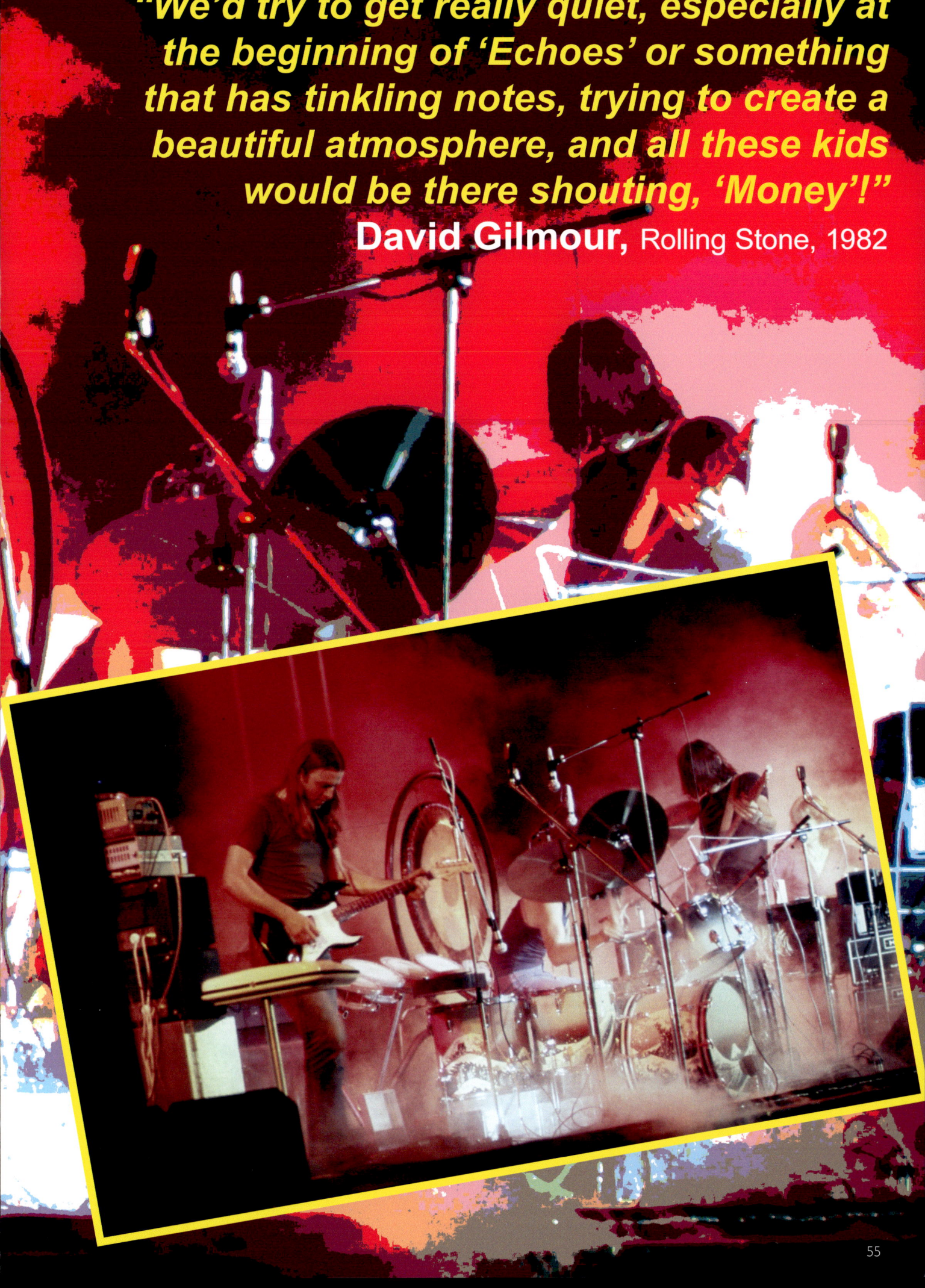

"We'd try to get really quiet, especially at the beginning of 'Echoes' or something that has tinkling notes, trying to create a beautiful atmosphere, and all these kids would be there shouting, 'Money'!"

David Gilmour, Rolling Stone, 1982

22 June 1974: The day after their show at the Palais des Expositions in Dijon, France the band enjoyed a game of football.

Roger Tillberg (Alamy Stock Photo)

The Animals album was released, 21st January 1977 and two days later the tour billed as "In The Flesh" started in Dortmund, West Germany.

Photos: Laurens van Houten (Frank White Photo Agency)

Photos: Laurens van Houten (Frank White Photo Agency)

Photos: Laurens van Houten (Frank White Photo Agency)

Rick Wright with his son Jamie in Munich, February 1977

The Animals tour included five nights at London's Wembley Empire Pool. This sequence of photos were taken by freelance photographer Steve Emberton whose work appeared regularly in *Record Mirror* and *Sounds*. As was invariably the case in those days, photographers like Steve were often requested to shoot a concert and then select the best one for publication. As was normally the case, the rest of the photos never got developed. As such this selection has never seen the light of day before and Steve dug out the original negatives for this publication.

Photos: Steve Emberton

"It's great when everything works together. We've been doing it for quite a long time now, right from the beginning with the light show, which was a haphazard affair, obviously. But we've been interested in doing more than just playing onstage. It's great fun when it works. It doesn't get in the way of the music, that's not the right expression. It just limits the amount of improvisation. It imposes a discipline, but within that framework you can still perform and improvise just as well."
Rick Wright, 4 November 1978

Snowy White who was brought in for the tour on the recommendation of Kate Bush's manager Hilary Walker. Snowy later joined Thin Lizzy and returned to working with Roger again for the 1990 Berlin Wall concert and has toured regularly with Roger throughout the subsequent decades.

Photos: Steve Emberton

Photos: Steve Emberton

Photos: Steve Emberton

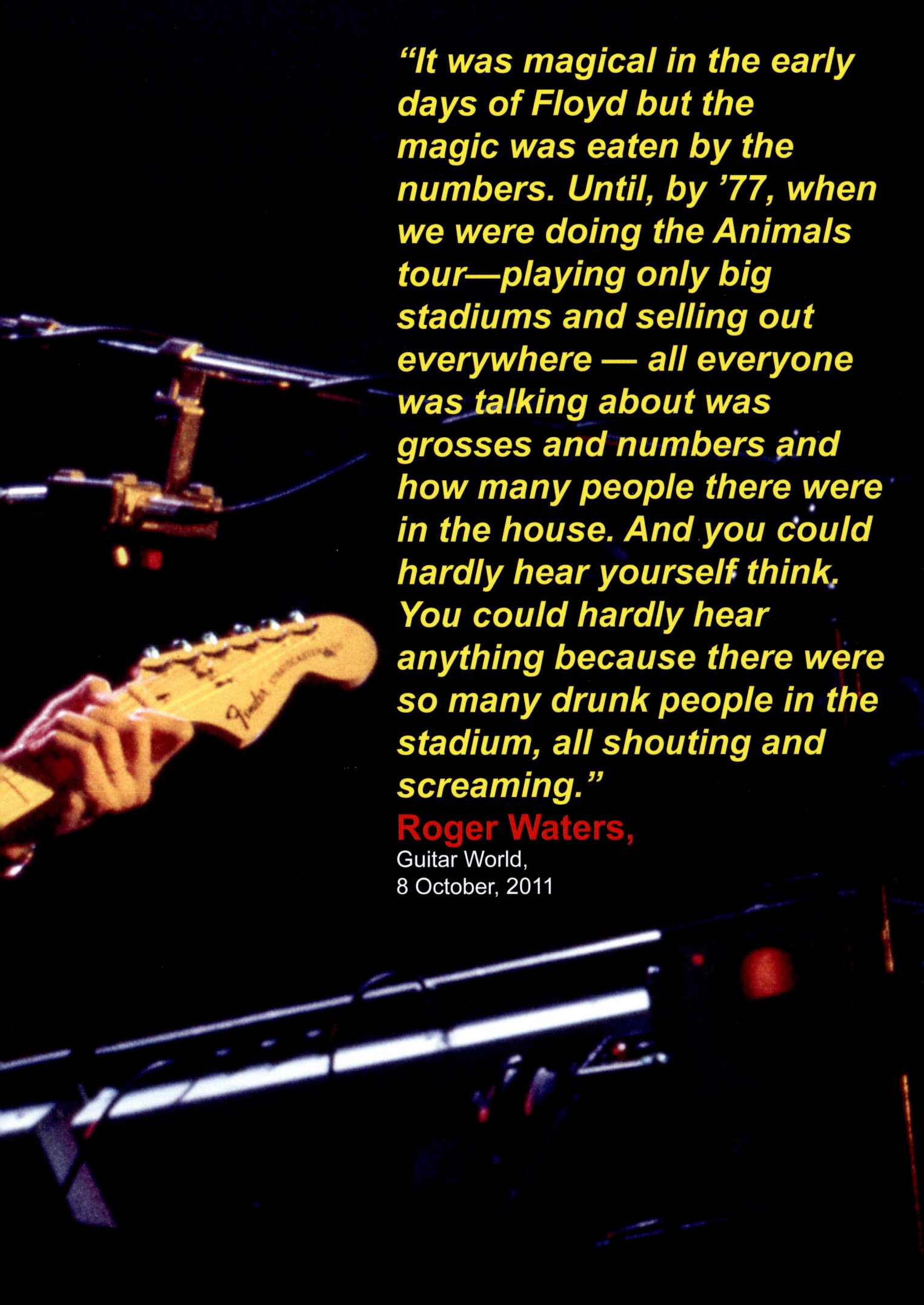

"It was magical in the early days of Floyd but the magic was eaten by the numbers. Until, by '77, when we were doing the Animals tour—playing only big stadiums and selling out everywhere — all everyone was talking about was grosses and numbers and how many people there were in the house. And you could hardly hear yourself think. You could hardly hear anything because there were so many drunk people in the stadium, all shouting and screaming."

Roger Waters,
Guitar World,
8 October, 2011

Photos: Steve Emberton

Following the 1977 In The Flesh Tour Nick Mason also recorded his debut solo album, *Nick Mason's Fictitious Sports*, in October '79 but it did not get released until May '81. It was a joint collaboration with American jazz musician Carla Bley who actually composed all the music. It was performed by her regular band with Mason as a guest, making it in effect a Carla Bley album in all but name.

"The team aspect of motorsport is vaguely similar, but the big thing is that when you are in a car you are totally on your own. The great thing in a band is that when things go wrong you can share it with three or four other people. Certainly the first rule of drumming is that if you make a mistake, turn round and look angrily at the bass player."
Nick Mason,
The Drummer's Journal,
Issue Six, Spring 2014

"The Floyd finished working at the end of July 1977, and we had no plans for the rest of the year. So David and myself, and Roger (Waters) had been wanting to do solo albums for a long time. While David and I were doing our solo albums, Roger was working on the next Floyd project. I can't say what it is, it's too early. It's a very definite idea but I wouldn't like to talk about it, basically, first because it's Roger's baby, his thing, and, two, it's too early to say we're doing this and this and this. In case it doesn't happen."
Rick Wright, 4 November, 1978

"It's true that we've made enough money to have time to really consider what we're doing rather than just rushing on and on and on. We don't have to work, but for how long, I don't know. I haven't really thought of that, actually. I haven't actually thought: 'Ah, I can stop now.' It never occurred to me."
Rick Wright, 4 November, 1978

"I think, looking back at what we were like when we started, and people I meet today, it's all to do with: 'I want to be successful. I want to sell lots of records.' It seems to me that's the goal. It was our goal, sure, when we started, simply to be very famous, successful. And after that one, you find you really have to sat back and think: 'Well, now what happens?' So the pressure then is on: what to write, what to play? And they're harder pressures than managers breathing down your neck to go out and earn a few bob."
Rick Wright, 4 November, 1978

David Gilmour in Los Angeles, 12th June 1978, promoting his debut solo album, recorded in February and March that year. Around the same time Rick Wright also recorded his debut solo album Wet Dream, which was released in September and included Snowy White.

Jeffrey Mayer (Pictorial Press Ltd / Alamy Stock Photo)

Another shot from the same period. "This album was important to me in terms of self-respect. At first I didn't think my name was big enough to carry it. Being in a group for so long can be a bit claustrophobic, and I needed to step out from behind Pink Floyd's shadow." *Circus*.

"But it's true that we're not doing this next Floyd project for money. We no longer have that pressure, since The Dark Side Moon, because that was the biggie. That pressure, to go out on the road because we had to financially, is over, but the other pressures that came, since Dark Side, were probably even harder to cope with, because it was a success. What does one do now?"
Rick Wright, 4 November, 1978

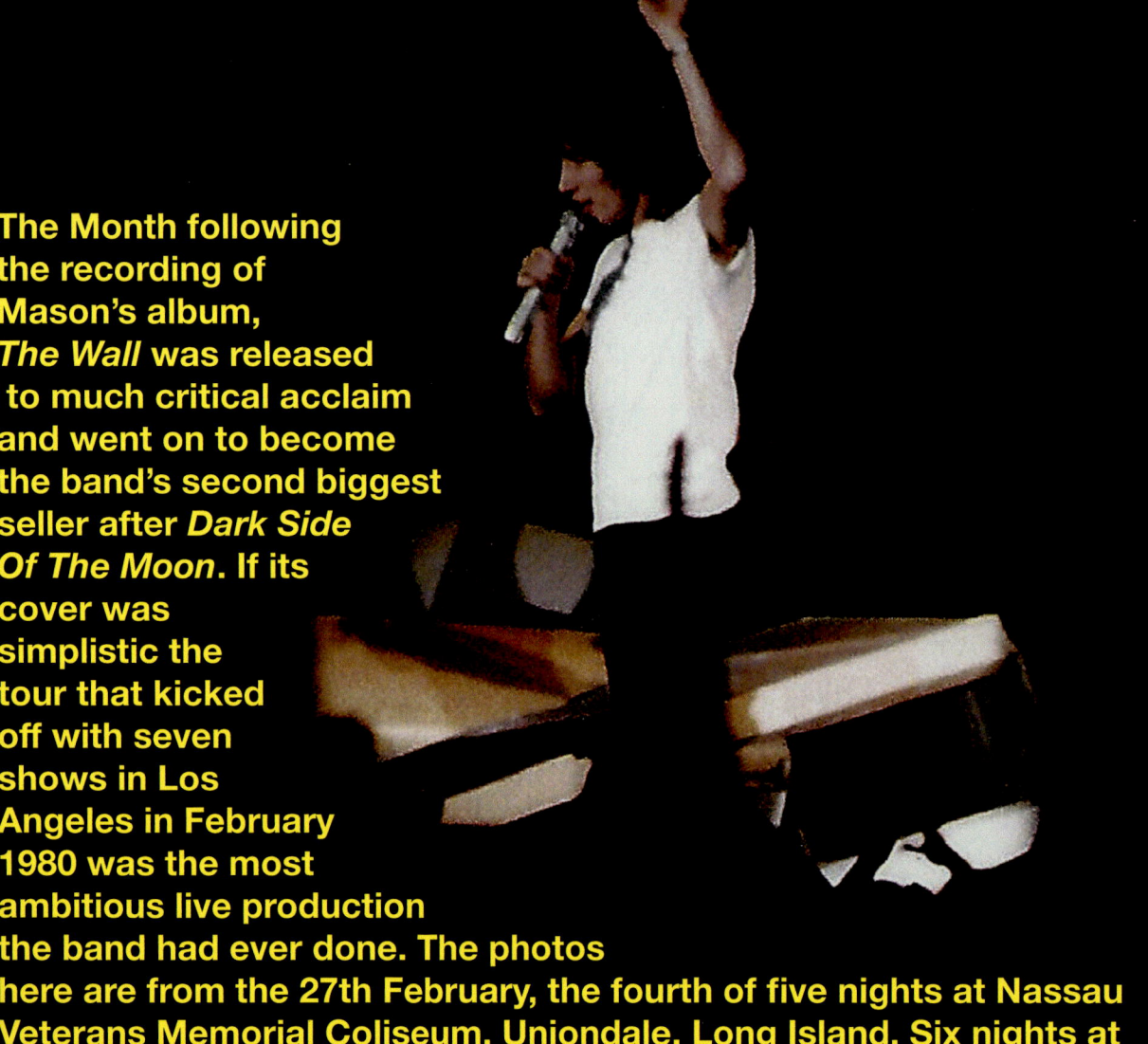

The Month following the recording of Mason's album, *The Wall* was released to much critical acclaim and went on to become the band's second biggest seller after *Dark Side Of The Moon*. If its cover was simplistic the tour that kicked off with seven shows in Los Angeles in February 1980 was the most ambitious live production the band had ever done. The photos here are from the 27th February, the fourth of five nights at Nassau Veterans Memorial Coliseum, Uniondale, Long Island. Six nights at London's Earl's Court were also played in the August.

Photos: Bill O'Leary (Frank White Photo Agency)

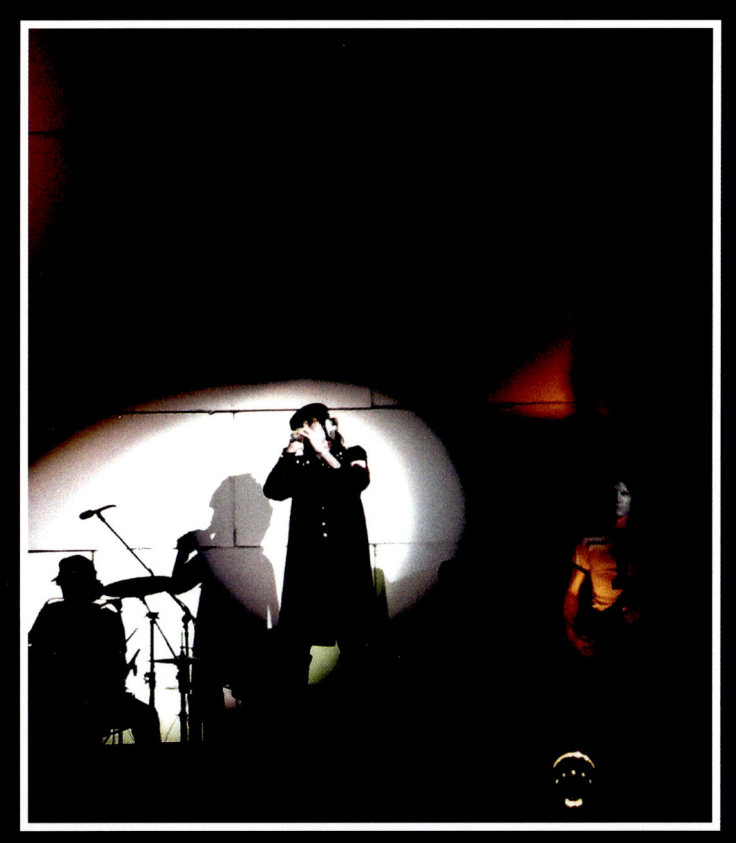

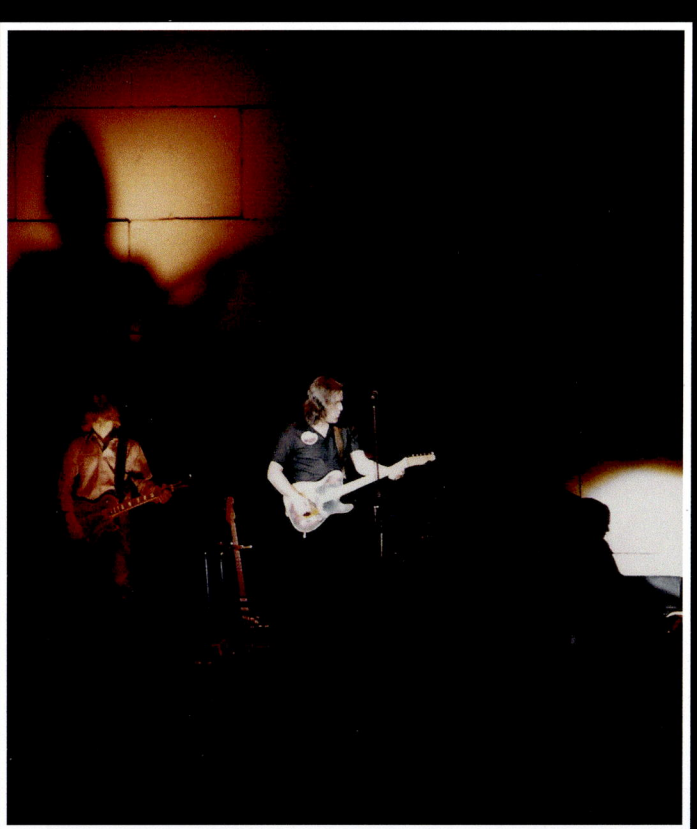

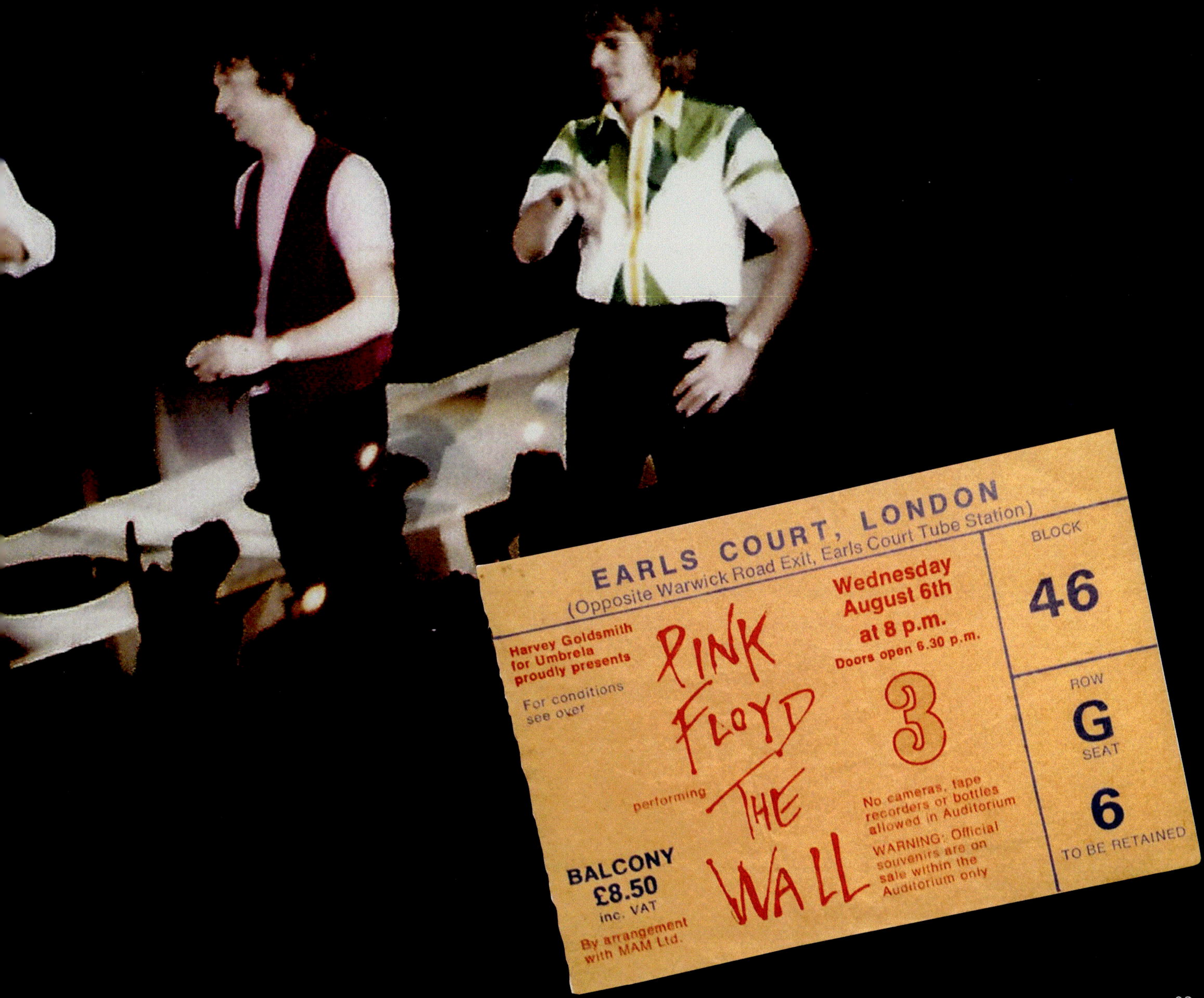
EARLS COURT, LONDON
(Opposite Warwick Road Exit, Earls Court Tube Station)
Harvey Goldsmith for Umbrela proudly presents
For conditions see over
PINK FLOYD
performing
THE WALL
Wednesday August 6th
at 8 p.m.
Doors open 6.30 p.m.
3
No cameras, tape recorders or bottles allowed in Auditorium
WARNING: Official souvenirs are on sale within the Auditorium only
BALCONY
£8.50
inc. VAT
By arrangement with MAM Ltd.
BLOCK
46
ROW
G
SEAT
6
TO BE RETAINED

The following year another thirteen performances were done. Five nights at London's Earl's Court took place in June and prior to that, eight nights at the Westfalenhalle, Dortmund, West Germany where these shots were taken.

Photos: Friedrich Stark / Alamy Stock Photo

"It was, for the most part, a typically British polite enmity that existed between them. They were obviously close on many levels. And there was an unadmitted mutual respect beneath all the arguing and bickering going on between them. But the tension was always present because there was a war between two basically dominant personalities. Each one had a need to express himself in his own style. And sometimes these styles were very different. Sometimes they approached the same piece of material from an entirely different point of view. So my job was often to be Henry Kissinger and run back and forth between the two of them, trying to arrive at a workable middle ground."
Bob Ezrin

"It's sad that these people think Syd's such a wonderful subject, that he's a living legend when, in fact, there is this poor sad man who can't deal with life or himself. He's got uncontrollable things in him that he can't deal with and people think it's a marvellous, wonderful, romantic thing. It's just a sad, sad thing, a very nice and talented person who's just disintegrated."
David Gilmour, Musician Magazine, December 1982

"Either you write songs or you don't. And if you do write songs like I do, I think there's a natural desire to want to make records. So, when I left Pink Floyd, I guess I had two, no three choices open to me: Not to do it anymore, which is daft as I was writing songs, although I suppose I could have written for other people, but I like making records; so I could either do it as Roger Waters or I could have got together with other people and said hey, why don't we start a band? But my view of bands had been jaundiced slightly by my previous experience, so I think that was something I never considered."
Roger Waters, Gold, 1992

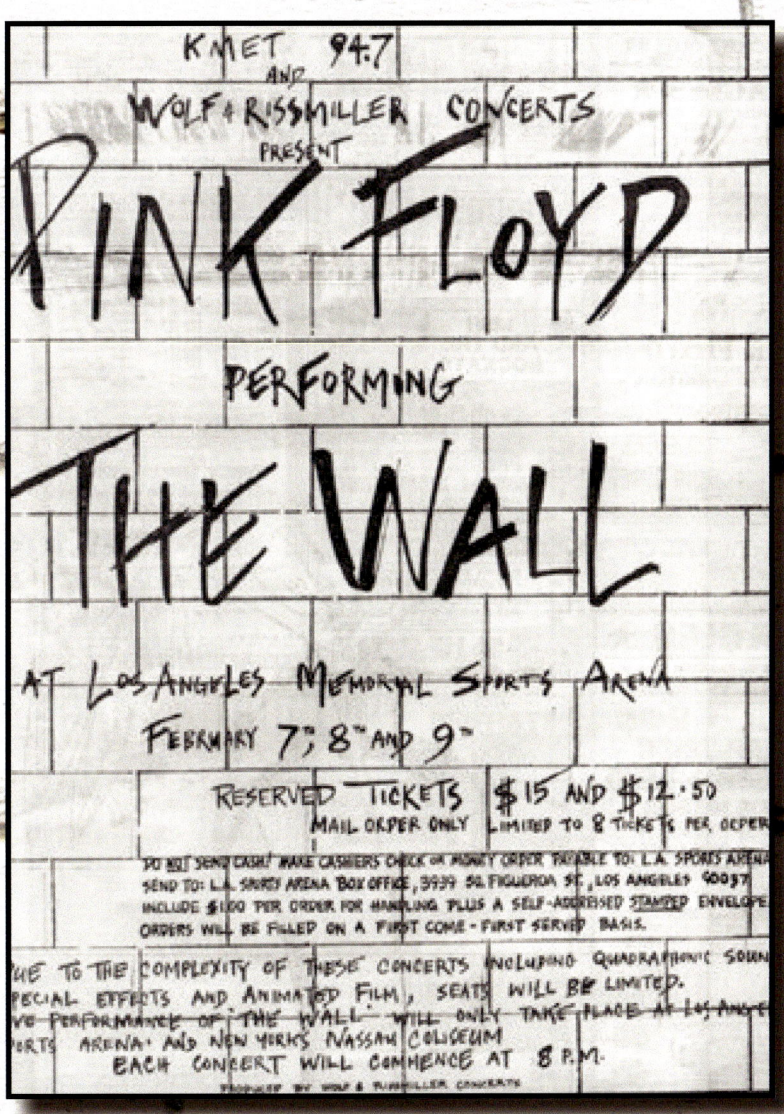

"I think that happiness resides somewhere between the extremes of personal, religious, and political. I think happiness resides where we understand someone else's point of view and needs. Happiness resides where we are not lost in the solitary dream."
Roger Waters,
November 2005

The early eighties was a turbulent time for the band. With Rick Wright having been dismissed and *The Final Cut* recorded in 1982 as a three-piece with additional musicians.

Roger with his then wife Lady Carolyne Christie at the BAFTA Awards 1983. That year he worked on recording *The Pros and Cons of Hitch Hiking* which was released in April 1984.

Dave Gilmour's second solo album About Face was released the month before and he toured in support of it but there was no activity under the Floyd name. In 1985 Waters toured the States in March and April and rumours that Floyd would perform at the massive Live Aid event, proved to be unfounded. As it turned out Gilmour did appear however, albeit providing accompaniment to Roxy Music's Bryan Ferry. Unbeknown to fans, Roger Waters left the band in late '85 and a bitter legal dispute followed as he claimed that Gilmour and Mason had no right to continue using the name.

Ilpo Musto / Alamy Stock Photo

By 1987 the situation was suitably settled. Gilmour and Mason, along with the returning Wright toured the States again as Pink Floyd in support of the A Momentary *Lapse Of Reason* album. Roger Waters simultaneously toured the same territory promoting his Radio *KAOS* album.

Following the fall of the Berlin Wall in 1989 Roger Waters staged one of the most ambitious concerts ever along with a host of other artists as he performed The Wall to an audience of 250,000 on a 25-acre site formerly occupying the no-man's land between East and West German at the Potzdamer Platz in Berlin. Here he can be seen with German band Scorpions who performed he opening number 'In The Flesh'.

Richard Wright, David Gilmour, Nick Mason at the Olympic Stadium, Munich, Germany, 4th August 1994 during Floyd's last ever tour which ran from March to October through North America and Europe.

"The very early days of Pink Floyd were magical. We played small auditoriums for entranced audiences, and there was a wonderful sense of communion. We got overpowered by the weight of success and numbers — not just the money but the size of the audience. I became very disenchanted. I had to make the choice of staying on the treadmill or making the braver decision to travel a more difficult path alone."
Roger Waters, USA Today, 1999

8th November 2004. Roger leaving the Cipriani Restaurant in New York with his then girlfriend Laurie Durning, who would become his fourth wife in 2012.

Rick Mackler / Globe Photos / ZUMAPRESS.com

"It's very hard to describe. It was such fun but it was also much more than that. It gave an enormous amount of pleasure, more really, to people who'd been fans for years - the people who have, essentially, paid for all our lifestyles. I know I've frittered mine away on old cars, maybe I should have invested it wisely."
Nick Mason, The Drummer's Journal, Issue Six, Spring 2014

Few imagined a reunion would ever be and it needed a special event to make it happen. The Live 8 Concert at Hyde Park in London, 2nd July 2005.

Antonio Pagano / Alamy Stock Photo

Antonio Pagano / Alamy Stock Photo

"The band? It's over. Reunited because of the good cause (Live 8), to get over the bad relationship, and not to have regrets."
David Gilmour, La Repubblica, February 2006

"It's actually quite emotional, standing up here with these three guys after all these years, standing to be counted with the rest of you. Anyway, we're doing this for everyone who's not here, and particularly of course for Syd."
Roger Waters

dpa picture alliance / Alamy Stock Photo

"I really wanted to establish that we are grown up enough to do things for one another. Also, it was in memory of all the good things that happened. We do have a reputation as being the band that always fought, but I think the reality is that a lot of bands do. Most of the time we spent together was terrific and recognition of that is important. For me personally, it was also important from the point of view of my children — seeing that adults can get together, set aside their differences and do the right thing for the right reason."

Nick Mason,
The Drummer's Journal,
Issue Six, Spring 2014

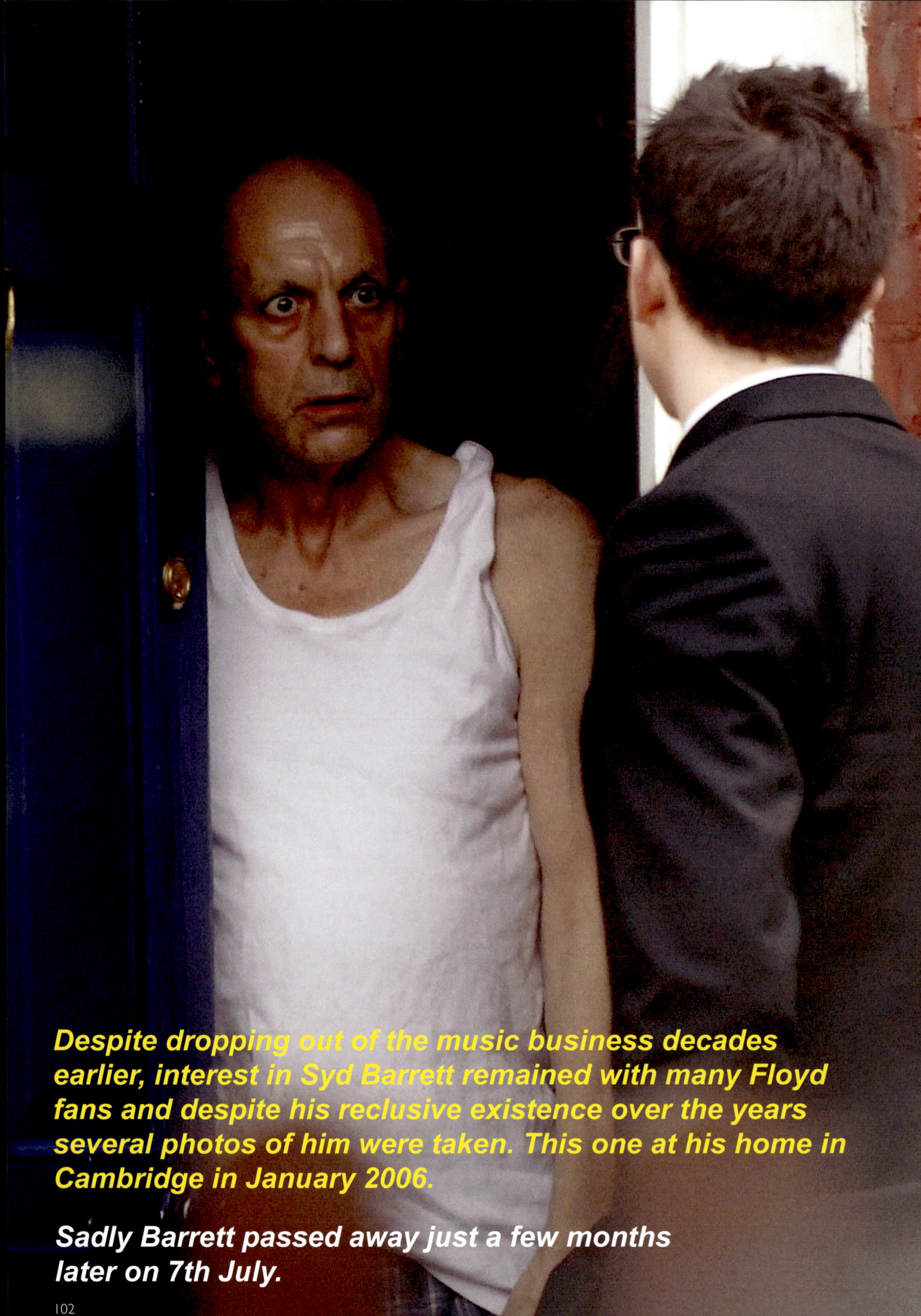

Despite dropping out of the music business decades earlier, interest in Syd Barrett remained with many Floyd fans and despite his reclusive existence over the years several photos of him were taken. This one at his home in Cambridge in January 2006.

Sadly Barrett passed away just a few months later on 7th July.

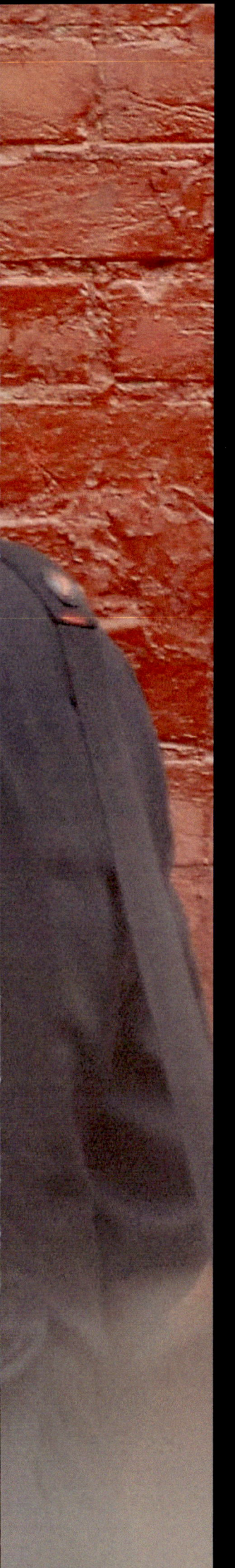

"I can't tell you how sad I feel. Syd was a major inspiration for me. The few times I saw him perform in London at UFO and the Marquee clubs during the '60s will forever be etched in my mind. He was so charismatic and such a startlingly original songwriter. Also, along with Anthony Newley, he was the first guy I'd heard to sing pop or rock with a British accent. His impact on my thinking was enormous. A major regret is that I never got to know him. A diamond indeed."
David Bowie

"He shaped the Floyd's sound, by his songs and playing and the way he sang. But when I went into the studio with them to produce 'Arnold Layne', Syd was diffident. He'd wander off, go outside and disappear. My memory of the control room was of Roger and, to a lesser extent, Rick and Nick, being present and having a lot to say."
Joe Boyd

"As time's gone on and I've worked with other musicians, I've realised more and more what a genius Syd was. That's not just some rosy glow for the obituaries. It's a reflection of how much influence he had and how Pink Floyd remained his band throughout, even after he'd gone and they were doing their own thing. The band revolved around him and his spirit remained central, even after he went."
Peter Jenner

"Syd seemed happy-go-lucky. He had impish girl-magnet looks, and was happy to play on it. He had a very attractive, sexy girlfriend, and she wasn't the only one he was seeing. Then a couple of months went by, when people talked about Syd taking an awful lot of acid. I saw him at the end of that period, sitting in a London street, and he'd lost all that spark. He became vacant-eyed, even when he was with you. I saw him like that when they played The Roundhouse, later in that summer of '67… the last time I saw him."

"The Syd that I knew vanished from this earth that spring of '67. I never really knew the other Syd. I had a lot of sadness about Syd in 1967. He was a great and very, very talented guy. And that guy went away. A long time ago."
Joe Boyd

"The late sixties were a key time in terms of profound changes in post-war society and opening new doors and breaking down the old order — and Syd was a vital part of that. He was one of the great songwriters of the 20th century, up there with Lennon & McCartney and Nick Drake."
Peter Jenner

"'See Emily Play' was on the radio the day before I heard that he had died. It made me laugh, but also made me realise the innocence of the time it was made. It was the silliest and most beautiful example of its time. If only he'd put the drug stuff back until he'd made a few more albums."
Ray Davies

"His songwriting was very English. It's ironic that the Floyd was named after two blues singers, as they set out to be a blues band. But because of Syd, their music is almost devoid of blues. His singing style is completely English, and the songs are of the jaunty, witty music hall type. He's a classic songwriter in the tradition of Ray Davies, Lennon and McCartney, at that crossroads of music hall and pop."
Joe Boyd

"Remember him as the madcap genius who made us all smile with his wonderfully eccentric songs about bikes, gnomes and scarecrows. His career was painfully short, yet he touched more people than he could ever know."
David Gilmour

David Gilmour performing on stage at the Piazza San Marco in Venice 11 August 2006 during his On an *Island tour.*

Nick Mason at the film premiere of *Mr. Bean's Holiday* at the Odeon Leicester Square, London, 25th March 2007.

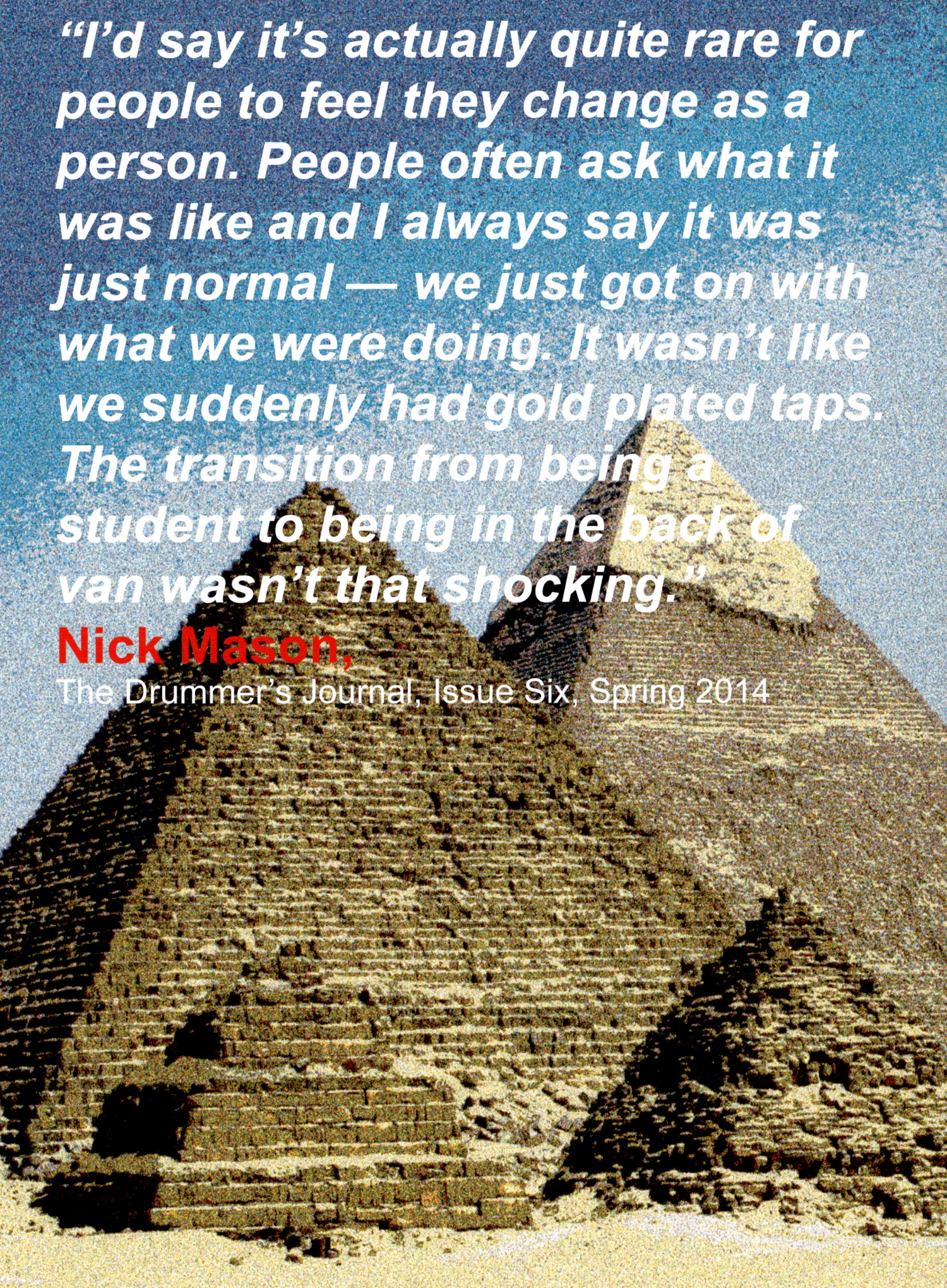

"I'd say it's actually quite rare for people to feel they change as a person. People often ask what it was like and I always say it was just normal — we just got on with what we were doing. It wasn't like we suddenly had gold plated taps. The transition from being a student to being in the back of van wasn't that shocking."

Nick Mason,
The Drummer's Journal, Issue Six, Spring 2014

Floyd reunited one more time (with Andy Bell of Oasis) at the Syd Barrett tribute concert held at The Barbican. London, England, 10th May 2007. Roger Waters chose to perform in a solo capacity although he was caught backstage with both Nick Mason and Rick Wright. Sadly any likelihood of additional reunions were scuppered when Rick Wright passed away on 15th September 2008.

"Losing Rick is like losing a family member – in a fairly dysfunctional family. He's been in my life for 45 years, longer than my children and longer than my wife. It brings one's own mortality closer. I'll remember Rick with great affection. He was absolutely the non-contentious member of the band and probably suffered for it. I wouldn't say he was easy-going, but he certainly never pushed to any aggravation. It made life a lot easier."
Nick Mason, Independent 19 September, 2008

"He was gentle, unassuming and private but his soulful voice and playing were vital, magical components of our most recognised Pink Floyd sound."
David Gilmour

"If there's something that feels like a legacy, it's Live 8 and the fact that we did surmount any disagreements and managed to play together. It was the greatest occasion."
Nick Mason, Independent 19 September, 2008

"It is hard to overstate the importance of his musical voice in the Pink Floyd of the 60's & 70's. The intriguing, jazz influenced, modulations and voicings so familiar in Us & Them and Great Gig In The Sky, which lent those compositions both their extraordinary humanity and their majesty, are omnipresent in all the collaborative work the four of us did in those times. Rick's ear for harmonic progression was our bedrock."
Roger Waters

Daimages Photo Agency/Alamy Live News

From 2010 Roger Waters started performing The Wall again with the added advantage of modern technology enhancing the shows no end. By 2013 the tour became the highest-grossing tour for a solo musician at almost half a billion dollars.

Roger in full flow Gradski stadion u Poljudu, Split, Croatia, 23 July 2013

Roger performing 'The Wall' at Manchester Arena, 16 September 2013

David Gilmour being interviewed at the Hay Festival, Hay-On-Wye, 27th May 2016

In 2016 Roger performed at the massive Desert Trip music festival at the Empire Polo Club in Indio, California on 9th October, 2016.

Daniel DeSlover/ZUMA Wire/Alamy Live News

20th March, 2017. Nick Mason reunited with an Abbey Road Console at Bonhams, Knightsbridge. The console was still in working order and was to be sold by Bonhams at their TCM Presents Rock and Roll Through the Lens sale in New York on the 27th March.

Keith Larby/Alamy Live News

Roger Waters and Nick Mason during a press conference of the 'The Pink Floyd Exhibition: Their Mortal Remains' at the MACRO Museum in central Rome on 16th January, 2018.

"Were not a tribute band. It's not important to play the songs exactly as they were, but to capture the spirit. I hope different elements will appeal to different people. Something like our version of 'Bike' is one of the more difficult things we've tackled. And then there are things like 'Set The Controls For The Heart Of The Sun', just because it's one of my favourite things to play."
Nick Mason

In 2018 Nick Mason returned to the stage with his Saucerful of Secrets band paying homage to the early Floyd music.

Milan, Italy
20 September 2018
Nick Mason's live at Teatro degli Arcimboldi

© Roberto Finizio / Alamy Live News

These pages are the front and rear cover of the first edition of this book: A limited edition hardback (500 copies) with 3 prints in a bespoke, custom-made, presentation box with holographic block foil.

© Andy Bishop

"Obviously I accept there are people who want to go and see and hear this legend that was Pink Floyd, but I'm afraid that's not my responsibility. To me it's just two words that tie together the work that four people did together. It's just a pop group. I don't need it. I don't need to go there. I'm not being coy or difficult, I just think that at my age I should do whatever I really want to do in life."

"And to do it without Rick would just be wrong. I'm all for Roger doing whatever he wants to do and enjoying himself and getting the joy he must have had out of those Wall shows. I'm at peace with all of these things. But I absolutely don't want to go back. I don't want to go and play stadiums… under the group banner. I'm free to do exactly what I want to do and how I want to do it. I don't know if it's as good as Pink Floyd or worse than Pink Floyd or better than Pink Floyd. I don't give a shit. It's what I want to do and it's what I will do.

David Gilmour, Classic Rock, 12 August, 2015